For Nicholas
R.M.

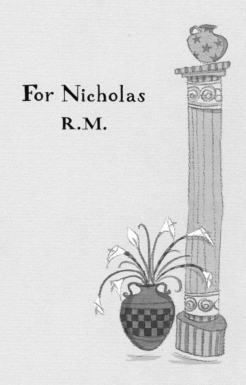

THE TALE OF

First published 1995 by Walker Books Ltd
87 Vauxhall Walk, London SE11 5HJ

10 9 8 7 6 5 4 3 2 1

Text © 1995 Jan Mark
Illustrations © 1995 Rachel Merriman

This book has been typeset in Tobias.

Printed in Italy

British Library Cataloguing in Publication Data
A catalogue record for this book is available
from the British Library.

ISBN 0-7445-3702-9

Asmodeus   The dog of Tobias

The Tale of Tobias is taken from the Apocrypha, a collection of Biblical books
included in the ancient Greek and Latin versions of the Old Testament.

TOBIAS

retold by JAN MARK   illustrated by RACHEL MERRIMAN

Tobit   Anna   Azarias   Sarah   Raguel

WALKER BOOKS
AND SUBSIDIARIES
LONDON • BOSTON • SYDNEY

I am the dog of Tobias.
I have no name, I am only a dog.
But Tobias and **I** have seen strange
things together. Listen, I'll tell you the story.

Tobias lived with Anna his mother and his father Tobit.
And me. I was a young dog then. While Tobit was rich
he gave food to the hungry and clothes to the poor.
He shared his money with those who had none.

But the King was angry with Tobit and took away all he had. So then Tobit and Anna were poor, and Tobit was blind. They had no money except for what Anna could earn. Times were hard. Things looked bad for us all.

Then **T**obit remembered that when he was rich he left some money with a friend in a city, far away. **S**o he said to **T**obias: "**G**o to my friend in that faraway city, and bring

the money home. The road is long and you may meet
bandits. Hire a man to go with you and when you come
home with the money we will pay him good wages."

Tobias met a man whose name was Azarias, and Azarias said: "I will go with you to that faraway city and bring the money home."

Tobias thought he could trust Azarias, but I was
not so sure. When I first saw him I thought he was
a great bird with wings. But I am only a dog.

Tobias said goodbye to his father Tobit and Anna his mother, and went away with Azarias. And I went with them. We walked all day and when night fell we stopped to camp by a river.

I saw a great fish and barked and ran in circles. Azarias said to Tobias: "Catch the fish and we will have supper." So Tobias caught the fish and Azarias said to Tobias: "Cut up the fish and keep the guts. We will roast the rest and eat it for supper." I thought: That is strange. I am the one who gets the guts. But I said nothing. I am only a dog.

Next day we walked in the hot sun and the fish guts smelled good to me. Tobias said to Azarias: "Why are we carrying fish guts?" Azarias said to Tobias: "If we meet a demon, burn the heart of the fish and the liver of the fish and the smoke will drive that demon away. But keep the gall of the fish," said Azarias. "It will make a blind man see."

I thought: Tobit is blind, but no one asked me what I thought. I am only a dog.

We walked on and the sun grew hotter and the guts smelled stronger. Then darkness fell. Azarias said to Tobias: "Tonight we will stay with a man called Raguel. He has a daughter called Sarah and you are going to marry her." I thought: That is strange. How can Azarias know such a thing? But no one asked me what I thought.

Tobias said to Azarias:
"I have heard about Sarah. She is beautiful
and good and I am sure I shall love her, but
she has had seven husbands and they are all
dead. One after another they died
on the night they were wed."
Azarias said to Tobias:
"All men love Sarah
and so does a demon,
Asmodeus. He is the
one who killed her husbands,
but he will not kill you." And
Azarias said to Tobias:
"You shall marry Sarah and
you shall not die."
And I thought:
How does he know?

That night we came to
the house of Raguel.
He greeted us kindly
and called us in, and we
all sat down to eat.
And Azarias said:
"Raguel, Tobias my
friend has come to
marry your daughter."
Raguel said to Tobias:
"If you marry my
daughter you will die
before morning."

But Azarias said:
"He will not die."
Then Sarah came in and
Tobias said: "I love you
already. Let us be wed."
And Sarah said:
"I love you already, but
if we are wed you will
die before morning."
But Azarias said to
Tobias: "You will not die.
Remember the fish guts."

So they were wed and went to bed. I lay down at the door. I saw the demon creep inside, and I heard Sarah scream.

But Tobias put the heart of the fish and the liver of the fish upon the fire, and the smoke rose up and the demon ran out, and was never seen again.

I went to find **Raguel**.
He was out in the garden
digging a grave for **Tobias**.
I danced in circles and
shouted: **Stop! Tobias** is
alive and the demon has
fled. But he did not know
what **I** was saying.
I am only a dog.

Next day Tobias and Sarah came out and said: "The demon has fled and we shall live happy ever after." Then Raguel gave a wedding feast that lasted fourteen days.

So Azarius said to Tobias: "You stay here to feast with Sarah, and I will go to that far city and fetch the money that Tobit left with his friend."

The city was far, far away,
but Azarias left and came
back in one night and
one day. I thought:
That is strange, but
no one asked me what
I thought. You know why.

Then we went home,
Tobias and Sarah,
Azarias and me.
And when we came
to the house out ran
blind Tobit, saying:
"Is that you, my
son?" And Azarias
said to Tobias:
"Do not wave, he
cannot see you.
But remember the
gall of the fish."

So **Tobias** ran to his father and put the **gall** of the fish on his eyes.

And **Tobit** yelped like a puppy and said: "**That hurts,**" and rubbed his eyes. And he could see again.

Then **Tobias** said: "**Mother**, **Father**, here is my wife **Sarah**, and the money you sent me to fetch. **W**e owe everything to our good friend **Azarias**. **L**et us give half of the money to him."

But **Azarias** said: "**No**, **Tobias**. **I** was your friend but **I** am not **Azarias**. **I** came to help you when you were in trouble because you are all good people.

"I am Raphael, one of the seven holy angels in Heaven. Give thanks to God, for it was He who sent me."
And then he went away.
I knew I was right about the wings.

So now **I** am old and **I** sit in the sun at the feet of my master **Tobias**. **I** am only a **dog**, but once **I** walked with an angel.